Portland Head Lighthouse, Cape Elizabeth, ME – In existence since 1791, Portland Head light is one of the most popular and often visited lighthouses in New England, towering 80 feet tall. The keeper's dwelling houses a museum. In addition there is a small gift shop on the grounds.

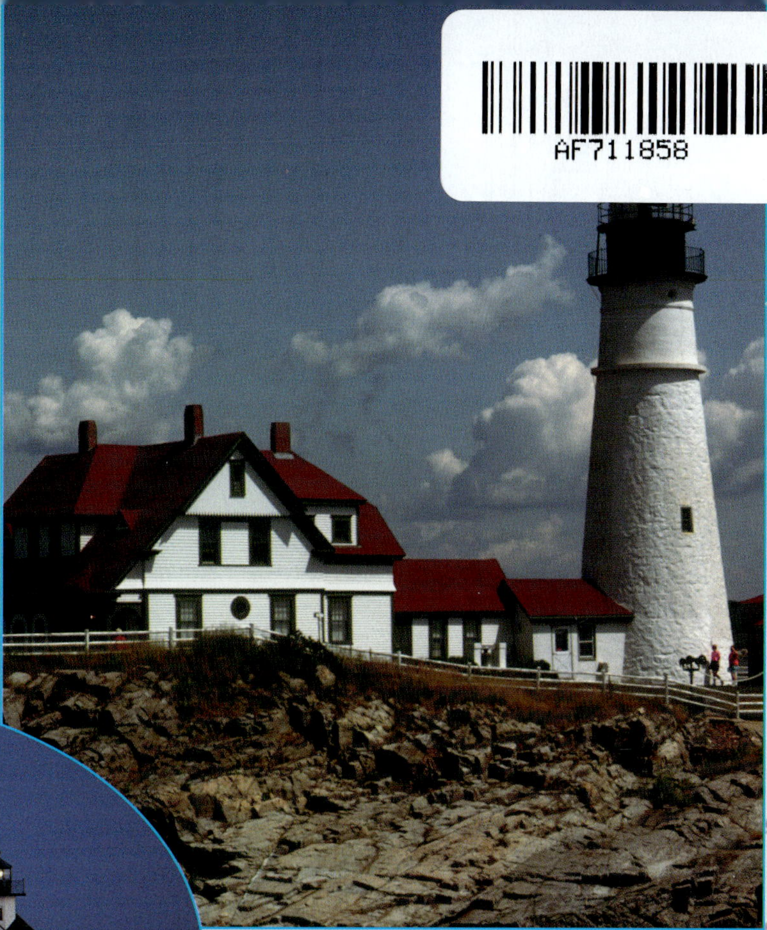

The Cuckolds Lighthouse, ME – is situated at the entrance to Booth Bay Harbor. Its octagonal light began as a fog signal station in 1892.

Pemaquid Point, ME – Now the site of the Fisherman's Museum. Its 38-foot high tower originally held Argand lamps, replaced by a fourth order Fresnel lens in 1856. *(photo courtesy of Bob Faucher)*

Wood Island Lighthouse, ME – First established in 1808 then automated in 1986. Its keeper's quarters are attached by a covered walkway.

Two Bush Island, ME – This picturesque lighthouse from 1897 shines a white light with a red sector flashing every five seconds.

Curtis Island Light, ME – Its 25-foot tower heralds the entrance to Camden Harbor. So named for publisher Cyrus Curtis who donated the land and building to Camden Harbor.

Owl's Head Lighthouse, ME (above and right) – With a history of many wrecks during severe thunderstorms, Owl's Head lighthouse is visible from 16 miles away.

Indian Island Lighthouse (Graves Light) ME – Built in 1874 of brick, it is now privately owned.

Cape Neddick, ME – Also known as "The Nubble" light, this lighthouse rests 88 feet above the water and has a fourth order Fresnel lens.

Spring Point Ledge Light, ME – This "spark plug" type lighthouse is constructed of iron plate with brick lining.

Marshall Point, ME – The light was leased to St. George Historical Society. The keeper's dwelling now houses a museum and connects the lighthouse to land by a wooden walkway.

Hendrick's Head Light, ME – Now a Privately owned residence.

West Quoddy Head Lighthouse, Lubec, ME – Sitting on the eastern most point of land in the United States, this photogenic red and white banded tower is one of the most popular lighthouses along the Maine coastline.

Cape Elizabeth Lighthouse, ME – Towering 67 feet in height, the original second order Fresnel lens has been removed and is on display at Cape Elizabeth Town Hall.

Whitehead Light, ME – Built in 1852, this active 41-foot tower harnessed wave power from Penobscot Bay to activate its original fog signal bell. Its original third order lens is housed at the Shore Village Museum in Rockland.

Rockland Breakwater Lighthouse, ME – Built after construction of a breakwater, busy waterway traffic makes this light and fog horn signal essential for the safe navigation into Rockland Harbor.

Hospital Point (Range Front) Lighthouse located near Beverly, MA, has a unique square pyramidal design.

Cleveland Ledge, MA – Situated in Buzzards Bay, the reinforced concrete structure has a 70-foot tall tower.

Minots Ledge near Cohasset, MA – This lighthouse was constructed of interlocking granite blocks, some weighing as much as two tons.

Brant Point, MA – In 1746, this was the second lighthouse to be built in the United States. In more than two and a half centuries, the lighthouse has been rebuilt 8 times.

Cape Pogue, MA – Rebuilt three times and moved twice, this Chappaquiddick Island lighthouse is built of stone and wood shingle.

Gay Head, Martha's Vineyard, MA – Its powerful first order Fresnel lens shines from a height of 170 feet above the water.

East Chop, MA – This cast iron construction on Martha's Vineyard is also called "Telegraph Hill."

West Chop, MA – is home to this beautiful active 84-foot tall lighthouse.

Edgartown Lighthouse, MA – The original tower was seriously damaged during the hurricane of 1938. This tower, built in 1939 was its replacement.

Eastern Point, MA – Built on Ten Pound Island inside the Gloucester Harbor, its fourth order Fresnel lens flashes every 5 seconds.

Nobska Point, MA – With its lantern 87 feet above sea level, this white cylindrical iron lighthouse is occupied by the Coast Guard. The grounds are open to the public.

Now a museum, the **Nantucket Lightship** was purchased by the Intrepid Sea and Air Museum and its new home will be in Boston.

Cape Ann, MA – Excursions by boat are possible to Thacher Island, named for a reverend who was shipwrecked here in 1635.

Buzzards Bay, MA – A "Texas Tower" type structure with a helicopter landing pad. Like many others this light employs a two-bulb system, so when one bulb burns out, it is automatically replaced by the second.

Graves Lighthouse, MA – This 113-foot tower built of granite blocks has withstood the harsh weather of the Boston Harbor since 1905.

Boston Light, MA – Located on Little Brewster Island it was the first light station in the United States, established in 1716. The existing tower was constructed in 1789 after the British burned the original tower during the Revolutionary War.

Rose Island, RI – Restored in recent years to its 1912 appearance, it rests on its 16-acre island. Accessible to visitors by boat from Fort Adams.

Newport Harbor Light (Goat Island), RI – Standing 35 feet, the octagonal tower originally had a residence attached until 1922 when it was struck by a submarine, requiring the dwelling to be dismantled.

Watch Hill Light, RI – The second lighthouse built in Rhode Island, it overlooks Fishers Island Sound.

Sakonnet, RI – The light was destroyed in 1954 by a hurricane. Restoration took place in 1985.

Castle Hill Light, RI – Narranganssett Bay, East passage. Built on granite blocks, this active tower once had a keeper's dwelling which was destroyed in 1938.

Beavertail, Conanicut Island, RI – America's third lighthouse, built in 1749. A fourth order Fresnel flashes a green light.

Point Judith, RI – Situated among one of the most dangerous areas of the Atlantic Coastline. The lighthouse was the first Rhode Island radio beacon established in 1931.

Block Island (North), RI – Since it's inception in 1829 this lighthouse has been moved one quarter mile inland. Visitor access is possible by ferry.

Block Island (South), RI – Stands a towering 201 feet above sea level. Threatened by erosion it was recently moved 220 yards inland as indicated by the arrow.

Great Captain Light, CT; Sheffield Island Light, CT; Stonington Harbor Light, CT; Block Island (North) Light, RI; Morgan Point Light, CT; Old Field Point Light, CT and Plumb Island Light, CT all used similar structures for their lights. Three are shown here (left, right, and directly below). Stonington Harbor Lighthouse is now a museum.

Latimer Reef, CT – The existing white tower was constructed in 1884 and is identified by a brown band.

New London Ledge Light, CT – Surrounded by Long Island Sound, this three story mansion warns ships away from the shoals near the mouth of the Thames River.

Stratford Shoal, CT – Built in 1877, this octagonal tower rests atop the keepers dwelling, and utilizes solar power to shine its beam 60 feet above Long Island Sound.

Lynde Point (Saybrook) Lighthouse, CT – Built on a granite pier of brownstone blocks, this octagonal white tower with red and grey lantern beams its fifth order lens from 71 feet above the water.

Stratford Point Light – an active lighthouse, built in 1881 of brick and cast iron. The lantern was replaced in 1990.

Saybrook Breakwater Light, CT – Connecticut River/Long Island Sound, this cast iron structure remains an active aid to navigation standing 48 feet above the water.

New London Harbor, Lighthouse, CT – This 89-foot tall octagonal structure was built in 1801.

Montauk Point Light, NY – now towering 160 feet above sea level, the building of the original tower was authorized by George Washington, and fitted with thirteen whale oil lamps.

Orient Point Lighthouse, NY – also referred to as the "Old Coffee Pot," its light is seen from fifteen miles at sea.

Fire Island, NY – Before restoration (left) this lighthouse was regarded as the most important beacon for New York bound steamers coming from Europe. Currently, Fire Island Lighthouse is part of the Fire Island National Seashore.

Statue of Liberty, NY – President Grover Cleveland turned Lady Liberty over to the Lighthouse Board after it was dedicated in 1886. The lighthouse was first lit later that same year.

Eaton's Neck, NY – Extremely well built by John McComb, Jr. in 1799, this lighthouse remains 144 feet above the water after two centuries.

Faulkner Island Lighthouse, CT – With its original 1802 tower, this solar powered lighthouse was the site for early fog signal experiments. It is now a bird sanctuary.

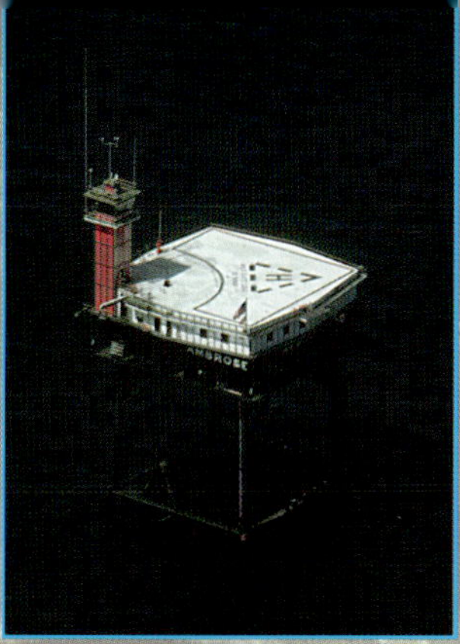

Ambrose Channel, NY – This "Texas Tower" replaced the station's lightship in 1967. The pile structure boasts a helicopter landing pad and electronic communications equipment.

Jeffrey's Hook, NY – made famous by the children's story *The Little Red Lighthouse and the Great Gray Bridge* by Hildegarde Hoyt Swift, Jeffrey's Hook guided navigators up the Hudson River until the construction of the George Washington Bridge in 1913. It is now part of Fort Washington Park.

Old Field Point , NY – located on Long Island's north shore, now owned by the town.

Cedar Island Lighthouse, NY – No longer operational, the light served a substantial purpose to whalers sailing toward Sag Harbor. It had several private owners before being turned over to the Suffolk County Historical Trust in 1984.

The building of **Race Rock, NY** was a monumental engineering feat, with tons of building supplies being ferried in violent water conditions, and masons working underwater. Together with the talents of construction foreman Captain Thomas Scott, F. Hopkinson Smith was the engineer, who also penned a novel about the construction of Race Rock Light titled *Caleb West, Master Diver.*

Execution Rocks, NY – Visible from Sands Point, NY - Execution Rocks was named for the revolutionary war practice of chaining prisoners to the rocks and leaving them to die at high tide.

Old Sands Point Lighthouse, NY – First established in 1809, this brownstone structure is now a privately owned residence.

Coney Island, NY – This steel pile skeletal structure of 70 feet in height was only recently automated in 1988, ending the career of the last civilian lighthouse keeper in the U.S.

Stepping Stones, Long Island Sound, NY – Placed on the outer edge of the reef this square lighthouse rests atop a granite and concrete pier. Though still active, it is not open to the public.

Valcour Island (Bluff Point) Lighthouse, NY – Built of blue limestone and timber. Although no longer active, this Lake Champlain landmark is accessible by boat from Adirondack State Park.

Colchester Reef Lighthouse, VT – Established in 1871, and originally on Lake Champlain. This lighthouse was moved to the Shelburne Museum in 1952. The sidewheeler Ticonderoga is in the foreground.

Kingston Light, NY – Located at the intersection of Rondout Creek and the Hudson River. Open to the public, it exhibits the history and heritage of the lighthouses and their keepers along the Hudson.

Hudson-Athens (Hudson City) Lighthouse, NY – Beginning service in 1874 this structure was built with a square light tower attached to the house. Now automated, it shines 49 feet above river level.

Esopus Meadows, NY – Abandoned by the Coast Guard in 1966. Curtains were painted on the boarded windows to discourage vandalism.

Absecon, NJ – Relocated to Atlantic City in 1963 for use as a park centerpiece. The lens is a first order Fresnel, but deactivated.

Sandy Hook, NJ – Remarkably, Sandy Hook withstood the Revolutionary War and centuries of weather since 1764. It remains the oldest lighthouse in continuous operation in the United States.

Barnegat, NJ – The lantern room rests 163 feet above the water and is fitted with a brilliant first order Fresnel Lens.

Twin Lights, Navesink, NJ – The fortress style towers were the site of the first Fresnel Lens experiments in 1841. In 1899 telegraph communication was also first used at this station during the America's Cup Races.

Cape May, NJ – This conical structure stands a towering 175 feet above sea level.

East Point, Maurice River Lighthouse, NJ – Badly damaged by fire in 1971 and restored nearly a decade later. The light was relit in 1980 after almost forty years of darkness.

Brandywine Shoal Light, Delaware Bay, NJ – The first American screw pile lighthouse, built in 1850.

North Breakwater Light, DE

Fenwick Island, DE – on the Maryland/Delaware border. Fenwick Island light guides the ships from 84 feet above the sea with its third order Fresnel lens.

Fourteen Foot Bank Lighthouse, DE – Built in 1886 this was America's first submarine type lighthouse structure.

Ship John Shoal, DE – Named for a vessel which ran aground here.

Delaware Breakwater Lighthouse is a "Spark Plug" Architectural-styled lighthouse and remains an active navigational aid.

Miah Maull Shoal Light, NJ – Operating on the North end of the shoal of Delaware Bay. This lighthouse is made of red cast iron with brick lining.

Located in the Harbor of Refuge, **South Breakwater Light** (Lewes Harbor) original tower was damaged by storm then rebuilt in 1926.

Concord Point Light – Located near Havre de Grace, **MD**, this is the oldest continually used lighthouse on the East Coast. Its most famous keeper John O'Neil was a veteran from the war of 1812.

Hooper Strait, MD – Standing 41 feet tall this lighthouse was moved from Tangier Sound to the Chesapeake Bay Maritime Museum.

The twin lights of Cape Henry, Virginia Beach, VA – The first lighthouse (left) was lit with fish-oil lamps in 1792. Its absence a dozen years earlier helped the Colonists resist a British Squadron of 27 ships. In 1870, it was feared that large cracks appearing would collapse the tower, and so it's companion (right) was built of cast iron and stands 100 yards to the southeast.

Assateague, VA – Originally the lighthouse tower was too low and too weak a light, to be effective. Equipped with a first order lens in 1867, its light can be seen for 19 miles. It is now part of the Chincoteague National Wildlife Refuge.

Smith Point, VA – Originally erected as an iron-framed tower lighthouse in 1802. The lighthouse saw several incarnations; as a lightship, then as a screw pile lighthouse, and finally after it was pushed over by ice in 1895, replaced again in the style of a concrete-filled, cast iron cylinder

Cove Point, MD – Marking the north entrance to the Patuxent River, the 51-foot tower received a fourth order Fresnel lens in the 1850's and is now automated.

New Point Comfort, VA – This octagonal tower is 63 feet tall and made of sandstone. Decommissioned by the Coast Guard in the 1950's, it was later restored in 1981 in honor of all locals who had died at sea.

Piney Point, MD – Abandoned and no longer lit, Piney Point was the first lighthouse built on the Potomac River.

Wolf Trap, VA – Floating ice in 1893 tore this lighthouse from its foundation. It was later found drifting toward the capes.

Cape Charles, VA – Located on Smith Island at the entrance to Chesapeake Bay, this towering lighthouse measures 191 feet in height. Its first order lens is on display at the Mariners Museum.

Thomas Point Shoals, MD – Located four miles south of Annapolis, the lighthouse was moved offshore in 1875 and into the bay and placed atop the shoals.

Drum Point Light, MD – Deactivated in 1962, this wood and cast iron dwelling was moved to the Calvert Marine Museum.

Baltimore Harbor Light, MD – Since 1908, this 38-foot tall lighthouse was first fitted with a fifth order lens, later utilized nuclear power, and is now a solar powered active aid to navigation.

Seven Foot Knoll, Baltimore, MD – Originally marking the entrance to Baltimore Harbor, this 1855 screwpile structure was moved to the city's inner harbor for use as a museum.

Old Point Comfort, VA – At 54 feet above water, this octagonal tower is the second oldest lighthouse on Chesapeake Bay. It was restored after damage it suffered during the Civil War.

Sandy Point Shoal Light, MD – Located in the Chesapeake Bay, this 37-foot high lighthouse is constructed of concrete and iron.

Turkey Point, Elk Neck State Park, MD – With a focal plane of 129 feet, the active 38-foot high masonry lighthouse was automated in 1947 after the last female civilian keeper in the Nation retired from her duties here. The lighthouse is accessible to the public.

Bodie Island, NC – First built in 1872, the present lighthouse, standing 170 feet tall is the third one on this spot. The horizontal bands distinguish it from Cape Hatteras.

Cape Hatteras Light – Located in Buxton, **NC** on the beautiful outer banks, this is one of the most famous and most visited lighthouses in the country. The structure was built in 1871 and is the tallest U. S. lighthouse at 208 feet. A "must visit" gift shop is at the restored keepers quarters.

Currituck Beach Light, NC – Located in Currituck County, this 162-foot brick tower has been left in its unpainted Natural Brick. The close-up gives you an idea of how many bricks it takes to build one of these structures.

Cape Lookout Light, NC – Built on a large barrier island off shore from Beaufort. It is still an active aid to navigation and open to the public as part of Cape Lookout National Seashore.

Ocracoke Island Light, NC – Ocracoke Island was made famous by the pirate Blackbeard and is home to this 65-foot white tower which houses a fourth order lens. Built in 1803, the structure is constructed of brick with a mortar surface.

Old Charleston Harbor (Morris Island Lighthouse) SC, – The land surrounding the lighthouse has eroded leaving just the lighthouse. It has survived hurricanes and earthquakes. Seen on the horizon is the **New Charleston Lighthouse**.

Hilton Head Lighthouse, SC – (Harbour Town) Privately built and owned as part of the Sea Pine Plantation.

Hunting Island Light, SC – Located in Beaufort County and situated on a lovely wooded island state park, this lighthouse is no longer in service.

New Charleston Harbor (Sullivan Island), SC – This lighthouse is triangular and has an elevator.

Oak Island Light, NC – The poured concrete is actually dyed so no painting is required.

Bald Head Light (Cape Fear), NC – "Old Baldy" is the oldest lighthouse in the state and is open to the public.

Georgetown Light, SC – This 87-foot tall tower built in 1867, is not open to the public, but leased to the South Carolina Department of Youth.

Cape Romain Light, SC – The present tower (octagonal in shape and black and white brick) was originally built in 1858, then deactivated in 1947. The bottom of an older tower (1827) remains.

St. Simons Island, GA – This 104-foot tall brick tower was built in 1872. The keeper's house has been beautifully restored and is well worth a visit. Both the tower and house are open to the public.

Sapelo Island Lighthouse, GA – This lighthouse is not open to the public.

Cockspur Island Lighthouse, GA – This 47-foot tall brick structure was built on a bed of oyster shells. At low tide, the lighthouse can be reached from Fort Pulaski.

Tybee Island Lighthouse, GA – Built in 1867, this 145-foot brick tower is open to the public, offering a museum and a terrific view of the Savannah River from the tower top.

Old St. John's River Light at Mayport , FL c.1858. Inactive. The keeper of its early days operated a complicated mechanism of enormous weights which hung inside the 80-foot brick tower, turning the Fresnel lens and offering itself as a powerful beacon of light.

Amelia Island Lighthouse , FL – Named for the daughter of King George II of England, this elegant 58-foot brick tower boasts a granite staircase and hand-hewn stairs brought by ship from England. Its lantern room holds an expensive French lens offering nearly 23 miles of visibility.

Cape Canaveral, FL – Erected in the mid-19th century, this active 139-foot light was relocated to its present site due to erosion in 1893. Its construction is unique; if necessary, the iron plates can be disassembled and moved, then reassembled.

St. Johns Light Station, FL – A thoroughly modern 64-foot concrete structure, this light station was once so isolated that a German submarine was able to drop 4 men ashore slightly south of here during World War II.

St. Augustine Lighthouse, FL – In the Nation's oldest city of St. Augustine, not far from the remains of a 16th-century brick watchtower erected by followers of Ponce de Leon, now stands an attractive spiral banded tower (measuring 161 feet high) on Anastasia Island. This old (1824) structure is Florida's first official lighthouse.

Ponce de Leon Inlet Lighthouse, FL – The second tallest in the United States. There are 203 steps to the top. On the grounds are 3 museums, a gift shop, video theatre and a Frensel Lens exhibit.

Hillsboro Inlet Lighthouse, FL – This iron pile structure was painted white at the lower half of its tower and black at its upper half to help mariners distinguish it from the neighboring Jupiter Inlet light.

Jupiter Inlet Lighthouse, FL – Built in 1860, a red brick tower of 105 feet, it rests on a 40-foot oyster shell mound left by prehistoric Indians.

Cape Florida Lighthouse (Key Biscayne, FL) – This 80-foot tower was repeatedly attacked during the Second Seminole War. A keeper's wife and children died at the hands of the indians here, as did the assistant.

In July 1996 the **Cape Florida Lighthouse, FL** was relit during Miami's Centennial Celebration.

American Shoal Light, FL – Like many Florida lighthouses, this was designed as an open structure to allow hurricane force winds to blow through.

Carysfort Reef Lighthouse, FL – The first screw pile lighthouse built in the Florida Keys in 1890, it was named for the ship Carysfort which was swallowed up at the reef in 1770.

Alligator Reef Lighthouse, FL – The schooner Alligator ran aground here in 1822, at a time when pirates preyed on passing vessels. The nine legged tower stands in five feet of water atop a coral rock formation.

Garden Key Light (Fort Jefferson in the Dry Tortugas), FL – Built in 1846 and never completed. Dr. Samuel Mudd was imprisoned here for unwittingly providing medical attention to President Lincoln's assassin. The fort was discovered to be slowly sinking and abandoned without being completed in 1874.

Loggerhead Key, FL – Built on an island named for the variety of turtles that once rested here. This Dry Tortugas lighthouse was mentioned in Ernest Hemingway's novel *To Have and Have Not* and it is the least accessible of Florida's lighthouses.

Sand Key – located 9 miles southeast of **Key West, FL**, the lighthouse keeper and her 5 children drowned in an 1846 hurricane at Sand Key. This tragedy gave way to a safer new lighthouse design using iron piles screwed into the seabed.

Sanibel Island Light (Ybel Point), FL – Prior to construction, its original parts sank in the Gulf of Mexico while in transit from New Jersey. However, nearly all the items were salvaged and the lighthouse was completed in 1885. The first keeper and his wife raised 13 children here.

Gasparilla Lighthouse, FL – established in 1927.

Old Port Boca Grande Lighthouse, FL – Located at the southernmost tip of Gasparilla Island, and built on steel stilts in 1890, it was recently restored after two decades of neglect. Now over a century later it provides an active aid to navigation with its original Fresnel lens.

Key West Lighthouse, FL – Possibly the farthest inland of any US lighthouse, Key West light was established in 1825 to safely guide vessels through one of America's most treacherous shipping lanes. Before its inception however, the area was popular with "wreckers" and pirates who tried to lure bountiful cargo ships onto the reefs with makeshift lanterns.

Crooked River Light, FL – Standing 115 feet above sea level in the small town of Carrabelle, this active skeleton tower replaces an earlier lighthouse situated offshore on Dog Island which sank into the bay as the result of a hurricane in 1873.

Saint Marks Lighthouse, FL – Standing a serene 82 feet high, and resting on a 12-foot deep limestone block base, Saint Marks lighthouse is home to a large wildlife refuge.

Pensacola Lighthouse, FL – Situated at the Pensacola Naval Air Station. The active 171-foot giant has withstood the Civil War, a lightning strike in 1875 and remained virtually unscathed during a Gulf Coast earthquake a decade later.

Anclote Lighthouse, FL – meaning "Anchor" was erected in 1887. Today it has been abandoned by the Coast Guard and remains unlit.

Egmont Key, FL – This light guards Tampa Bay with a visibility of 22 miles. The 85-foot high tower rests on the north end of the key.

Los Angeles Harbor Lighthouse, CA – Visible from San Pedro, this photo was taken from the pilot boat dock. This concrete cylindrical shaped structure was built in 1913.

Point Fermin, CA – Originally constructed in 1874, the structure was restored by the Sons and Daughters of the Golden West.

Point Vicente, CA – Established in 1923, this cylindrical tower with a focal plane of 185 feet stands guard in a complete 20th century station, constructed in a Spanish style.

Old Point Loma, CA – This picturesque Cape Cod dwelling supports a 40-foot tower. Its light is illuminated in the evening, but no longer an active aid to navigation. This lighthouse stands an impressive 462 feet above sea level. Operated by the Cabrillo Historical Society.

New Point Loma, CA – Because the Old Point Loma light was often above the cloud/fog layer, Mariners needed a lower light. The New Point Loma light was built in 1891 and has a focal plane of only 88 feet.

Point Conception, CA – This treacherous area of the California coast was said to be the graveyard of the Pacific.

Point Pinos, Monterey, CA – Completed in 1853, it has the distinction of being the oldest active lighthouse on the west coast.

East Brothers, CA – Now a bed & breakfast lodge, this active aid to navigation was built in 1874.

Point Arena, CA – At 115 feet tall, the current lighthouse replaces an earlier tower destroyed by the Great San Francisco Earthquake of 1906.

Point Cabrillo Light, CA – Built in 1909 of wood, this structure stands on a finger of land extending to the sea.

Point Sur, CA – The beautiful first order lens is on display at the Maritime Museum and History Center in Monterey CA. With the exception of the automation of the light this station remains unchanged since 1889. The site is now operated by the California Department of Parks.

Pigeon Point, Santa Cruz CA – Erected in 1872, The light atop its 148-foot tower can be seen for 18 miles. The lighthouse takes its name from the ship *Carrier Pigeon* which wrecked here during the mid-nineteenth century.

Saint George's Reef Light, CA – The most costly of all U.S. lighthouses to build, it is located six miles off shore, near Crescent City, California. This structure took ten years to build.

Battery Point, Crescent City, CA – Now a museum operated by the Del Norte County and accessible by foot at low tide, this 1856 granite building has withstood the enormous effects of the Pacific.

Point Reyes Lighthouse, CA – Part of the Point Reyes National Seashore, this light was built in 1870 and is open to the public during limited times. *(photo courtesy of John Gaffney)*

Point Bonita Lighthouse,CA – By San Francisco bay the 33-foot tower rests on a 100-foot rock cliff. This building was constructed in 1877. *(photo courtesy of John Gaffney)*

Tillamook Rock Light, OR – This lighthouse can be seen from Ecola State Park. Built in 1881, the structure was quite an engineering feat for the time. It is now owned by Eternity at Sea Columbarium.

Yaquina Bay Light, OR – Constructed in 1871 and made obsolete once Yaquina Head Light (below) was completed in 1874. The site is now a museum operated by the Lincoln County Historical Society.

Yaquina Head Light, OR – Built in 1874 on an outcropping three miles north of Yaquina Bay entrance, it contains a first order Fresnel lens (inset). The land is open to the public.

Heceta Head Lighthouse, OR – Probably the most recognized lighthouse on the west coast. Anyone who has taken the drive north of Florence since 1894 has seen it as they round the corner. The tower is only 56 feet tall, but the focal plane is 205 feet.

Cape Blanco Lighthouse, OR – It is the furthest west lighthouse of the continental United States. Located in what is now one of Oregon's state parks, it is Oregon's oldest lighthouse built in 1870.

Cape Arago Lighthouse, OR – As a testimony to the harsh Oregon weather, the present light is the third one at the site. Made of reinforced concrete, the present tower has lasted since 1934.

Coquille River Lighthouse, Bandon, OR – Constructed in 1896, the lighthouse was abandoned for many years (inset) before it was restored in the late 70's. Now part of Bullards Beach State Park.

Umpqua River Light, OR – Sixty seven feet tall with a focal plane of 165 feet, this lighthouse has a truly magnificent first order, 1894 Fresnel lens (shown above).

Cape Meares Lighthouse, OR – (1890) Because it is on a high bluff the actual tower is only 40 feet tall. It has a beautiful first order Fresnel lens (see lens on page 62).

Admiralty Head Light, WA – Built in 1903 and open to the public, the Island County Historical Society has this interpretive center where lighthouse lenses are on display.

North Head Light, WA – Built of stone and brick, this 65-foot tower was built in 1898 and is located in Fort Canby State Park with the lens on display.

Mukilteo Light, WA – Near the Mukilteo Ferry landing, this lighthouse is still an active aid to navigation and the building is a museum open to the public. This structure was built in 1906 out of wood.

New Dungeness Light, WA – Near Sequim, this lighthouse is one of the oldest on the west coast. Built in 1927, the tower is open to the public on weekends and is still an active aid to navigation.

Point Wilson Light, WA – Built in 1914, this concrete lighthouse is located in Fort Worden State Park.

West Point Light, WA – On Puget Sound as part of Discovery Park, this lighthouse was built in 1881 and constructed of brick.

Point No Point, WA – Built in 1879, this brick and stucco structure rises just 20 feet, but is high enough to help boaters through the fog for which Puget Sound is famous. Open to the public for limited hours.

Cape Disappointment Lighthouse, WA – Built above the bluff over looking the extremely hazardous Columbia River Bar, the site is occasionally open to the public (Fort Canby State Park).

Alki Point Lighthouse, WA – Another one of the small (37-foot tall) Puget Sound lights. Built in 1913, this light-house is still active.

Grays Harbor Lighthouse, WA – This 107 foot tower (above) was built in 1898, has an octagonal shape and a third order Fresnel lens. It is open to the public during limited times.

Destruction Island Lighthouse, WA – Built in 1891 from stone with iron plates, the tower is 94 feet tall with a focal plane of 147 feet. This photo was taken from a camp ground on Highway 101.

St. Joseph North Pier Inner and Outer Lighthouses, MI – These two towers act as both range and harbor lights. The Outer Light has a fifth order Fresnel lens. In 1907, after the pier was extended, the Inner Light was rebuilt. It houses a fourth order Fresnel lens.

Spilt Rock Light, MN – Rising regally 130 feet above Lake Superior, construction in 1909 required over 300 tons of materials to be lifted to the top of the rock. One reason a lighthouse and fog signal were badly needed was due to increasing ship traffic and the hazards ships faced while navigating because of iron ore deposits creating unusual magnetic attractions on their compass readings.

Duluth South Breakwater Outer Light, MN – This outer tower serves as a range light. Its original keeper's residence was built on shore rather than on the pier.

Duluth South Breakwater Inner Light, MN – Made of steel this active skeleton structure stands 67 feet tall, housing a white light from a fourth order Fresnel lens.

Grosse Point, Evanston, IL – Since 1873, this elegant and still active 90-foot tower with a red-trimmed lantern has served as a major landmark, warning vessels of nearby shoals in Lake Michigan.

Chicago Harbor Light, IL – This 48-foot tower is made of brick and cast iron. In 1919 the lighthouse was moved to the Chicago Breakwater.

Grand Haven, South Pier, MI – The elevated walkway is an effort to provide safer access to the light during the winter months.

Manitowoc Breakwater Light, WI – From its 10-sided lantern, this steel plated structure beams 51 feet above Lake Michigan with its fifth order Fresnel lens.

Sturgeon Bay Canal North Pierhead Light, WI – The original lighthouse design constructed here in 1899 did not allow for Wisconsin's strong winds and had to be altered before being virtually rebuilt in 1903.

Rawley Point, WI – One of the two watchrooms and a lantern were taken from a lighthouse which had been transplanted from Chicago in 1894.

Kewaunee Pierhead Light, WI – Atop the square tower rests an octagonal lantern which houses a rotating airport beacon. It can be seen standing 45 feet above Lake Michigan.

Marquette Harbor Light, MI – Situated on the north point of Lake Superior, this 40-foot high red brick structure was constructed in 1866.

Fort Gratiot (Lake Huron) Township of Fort Gratiot near Fort Huron, MI – The French built this fort in 1686. Over a century later Americans settled there and built the lighthouse at the head of the St. Clair River. It is the oldest lighthouse in Michigan.

Big Sable Point (Grand Point Au Sable), MI – First lit in 1867, the 112-foot brick tower and watchroom were later encased in steel plates.

Lorain Lighthouse, OH – Built in 1917 and currently deactivated, this 51-foot tall structure is shown here getting some of the foundation shored-up.

Vermilion, OH – This lighthouse is on the museum grounds at the Great Lakes Historical Society in Vermillion

Marblehead Light, OH – Formerly Sandusky Light, it stands 65 feet tall and was built in 1821. Marblehead is the oldest active lighthouse on the Great Lakes.

Frankfort Pier Light, MI – Many towns are proud of their lighthouses. Frankfort showcases theirs by posting the entrance to the town with a "lighthouse archway."

North Manitou Shoal Light, MI – Constructed in 1935, this square tower operates from a height of 63 feet, and replaces an earlier lightship.

Grand Traverse Lighthouse, MI – Nicknamed "Cat's Head" this is currently used as a museum.

South Manitou Island Lighthouse, MI – Rising 104 feet, this 126-year-old lighthouse is part of a museum with the national parks and can be reached by local ferry.

Wind Point Racine, WI – Guiding south-bound ships into Racine Harbor, this 108-foot white tower has a green lantern and red roof.

Point Betsie Lighthouse, MI – With only a 37-foot tower connected to the keeper's dwelling, it was considered one of the most important lights to guide vessels going north and south along the eastern shore of Lake Michigan.

Manistique East Breakwater Lighthouse, MI – In order to fill a void of over forty statute miles without a lighthouse between Seve Croix Point and Poverty Island, Manistique was built with a focal plane of 50 feet above Lake Michigan.

Dunkirk (Point Gratiot), NY – The 65-foot square tower was originally round, but later changed to complement the high Victorian Gothic style of the keeper's dwelling.

Fort Niagara, NY – This lighthouse boasts being the first American aid to navigation on the Great Lakes

Presque Isle Light, PA – Located on a peninsula on Lake Erie, the current lighthouse was erected in the 1870's.

Buffalo Lighthouse, NY – Past lighthouses of Buffalo have sustained significant damages from Ice and Vessels.

Milwaukee Breakwater Light, WI (left) – This steel frame white structure rests on a concrete pier. It's light shines 61 feet above Lake Michigan. **Milwaukee Pierhead Light, WI** (right) – At 42 feet high this red conical tower provides contrast to it's breakwater companion.

Superior South Breakwater (Wisconsin Point) Light, WI – The addition of this 1913 light tower and fog signal building rendered Minnesota's Point Lighthouse obsolete. Its electric beacon provides visibility to vessels from 70 feet above Lake Superior.

Cheboygan River Range Light, MI – While not active, this lighthouse has been restored. This light was an aid to traffic between Cheboygan and Mackinac Island.

Old Mackinac Point, MI – This 1892 lighthouse provided an invaluable service to ferryboats before the Mackinac Bridge was built in 1957.

Round Island, MI – With the construction of this lighthouse ships could better navigate the dangerous shoals in the channel between Mackinac Island and Round Island.

Cleveland Harbor (East Pierhead Light), OH – This 25-foot iron structure is solar powered.

Cleveland Harbor (West Pierhead Light), OH – This conical 67-foot tower on Lake Erie houses a fourth order lens.

Oswego West Pierhead Lighthouse, NY – In 1837 the lighthouse was moved to the end of the pier so that it would be more visible to ships entering the Oswego Harbor.

Port Austin Reef Lighthouse, MI – The square tower of yellow brick is an active aid to navigation. *(photo courtesy of Scott Clancy)*

Holland Harbor (South Pierhead), MI – The tower and twin-gabled keeper's dwelling are covered with steel plates. Its original sixth order lens was given to the Netherlands Museum.

Diamond Head Light, HI – Built in 1918 of concrete, the lighthouse has a third order Fresnel lens. This site is not open to the public, but can be viewed from Diamond Head Road.

Makapuu Point Lighthouse, HI – Built in 1909, this 46-foot concrete tower has the largest lens in America. While not open to the public, this lighthouse is an active aid to navigation.

Cape Hinchinbrook Light, AK – This beautiful lighthouse is perched at the entrance to Prince Williams Sound.

One of the many beacons lighting the inside passage.

Tchefuncte River Range Rear Light, LA – Near Madisonville, LA on Lake Pontchartrain. Built in 1867 this small (30-foot) brick structure has a distinctive black stripe. It is still operational.

Sabine Pass Light, LA – On the Louisiana side of the Texas/LA border, this weathered structure resembles a giant rocket. When in operation it had bright red and white stripes.

Mobile Middle Bay Light, AL – This hexagon structure has a small strobe where the lantern used to be. It is 54 feet tall and in the middle of mobile bay.

Galveston Jetty Light, TX – The lens was donated to the Galveston County Historical Museum. This photo was taken just prior to demolition.

Pass Manchac Light, LA – This 40-foot brick tower no longer has a light but is used as a daymarker for boaters on Lake Pontchartrain.

Sand Island Light, AL – South of Mobile Bay and now abandoned, the lens is in the Fort Morgan Museum. *Photo courtesy of Dave Brimblecom.*

Point Bolivar, TX – Built in 1873, this 116-foot lighthouse is on the north side of Galveston Inlet.

Cape Meares, OR

Makapuu Point

Former Fire Island Lens (first order) now at the Franklin Institute in Philadelphia.

Acapulco, Mexico

Wilson Promontory, Australia

Auckland Harbor, New Zealand

Cape Reinga, New Zealand

Portland Bill, England

Vancouver, British Columbia, Canada

British Columbia, Canada

Flat Holm, England

Sheringham Point Light, Canada